Original title:
Under Winter's Pale Moon

Copyright © 2024 Creative Arts Management OÜ
All rights reserved.

Author: Olivia Sterling
ISBN HARDBACK: 978-9916-94-590-2
ISBN PAPERBACK: 978-9916-94-591-9

Beneath the Canopy of Glimmering Stars

Snowmen wobble, hats askew,
With carrot noses, bright and new.
They dance a jig, they bust a move,
As children laugh and start to groove.

The squirrels plot in winter coats,
While penguins wear their tiny boats.
A snowball fights, a slippery race,
In frozen realms, we find our place.

Chilling Embrace of the Celestial Dome

Dreaming of hot cocoa's embrace,
Mittens and scarves in a playful race.
The snowflakes tease as they flutter down,
While penguins strut in their little town.

Icicles hang like a lazy crew,
As snowballs fly like birds that flew.
With rosy cheeks and giggles galore,
We chase the snowflakes, forever more.

Twilight Dreams Wrapped in Frost

Frosted trees wear glittering crowns,
While giggling children tumble down.
Hot chocolate spills, a marshmallow fight,
As eyebrows freeze, what a silly sight!

The moonbeams play peek-a-boo at night,
Bouncing off snow, oh what delight!
And as we slip on icy grooves,
We dance like stars, as winter proves.

Silvered Night: A Winter's Tale

Snowflakes giggle, they swish and sway,
In this chilly world, we come out to play.
The polar bear slips on a patch of ice,
And grins like we're all together, how nice!

With puffy coats and oversized gloves,
We tumble and roll like playful doves.
Under the sheen of a starry embrace,
Wondrous laughter fills this frozen space.

A Kiss of Ice and Light

The snowman dons a hat so grand,
His carrot nose can barely stand.
He winks at kids, a silly sight,
While sipping cocoa, pure delight.

The icy slide, a thrilling race,
We tumble down, a clumsy pace.
Laughter echoes, bright and loud,
As laughter wraps around the crowd.

Secrets Kept Beneath the Frost

The squirrels plot their nutty quests,
While penguins wear their cutest vests.
They scurry 'round in frosty cheer,
Planning dances by the pier.

The icy pond, a stage so slick,
The ducks all skate, a funny trick.
They quack and quibble, full of glee,
In winter's play, they feel so free.

Timeless Whirls of a Twilit Sky

The stars above have lost their minds,
They dance around, as if in binds.
Snowflakes swirl in dizzying twirls,
While giggling clouds, in white, unfurl.

A chilly breeze brings tickling laughs,
As snowflakes play in cosmic drafts.
The moon's a joker, glowing bright,
Tickling hearts with its silver light.

The Beauty Within the Stillness

Amidst the hush, a snowball flies,
A perfect shot! Oh, what a surprise!
With giggles ringing through the night,
As winter whispers, pure delight.

A game of freeze-tag in the night,
Kids dash about, their spirits bright.
The stillness hides such laughter sweet,
In every bounce of frosty feet.

Threads of Light in a Frostbound Realm

In the chill of the night, we laugh and we play,
Snowmen might wobble, but they brighten the way.
With carrot noses that wiggle and dance,
They'd break into jokes if given a chance.

Frosty the Snowdad, with boots that are bright,
Tripped over his scarf, what a comical sight!
He tried to catch snowflakes, slipped on some ice,
Said, "No harm, no foul, just a roll of the dice!".

The Calm Serenade in Winter's Grip

A penguin on skis, what a sight to behold,
Sipping hot chocolate in the icy cold.
He slides down the hill with a waddle so grand,
A snowball to dodge—oh, that wasn't planned!

The rabbits are dancing, they hop to the beat,
With oversized mittens on furry little feet.
They twirl and they spin in the frosty moonlight,
Chasing their shadows, what a silly sight!

Glowing Silhouettes Beneath A Night's Caress

There's a cat on a roof, looking proud with a pose,
He tips over a snowman, and down it goes,
With a "meow" that echoes, he struts with such glee,
While snickering softly at all the snow debris.

The owls in the trees, they hoot with delight,
As the wolves in the distance start howling at night.
They're laughing at snowflakes that tumble and glide,
While penguins throw parties, and squirrels can't hide!

A Tapestry of Shadows on the Snow

In shadows of night, the critters convene,
With a disco ball hanging, it's quite the scene.
They boogie on ice, in their fluffy attire,
While a beaver DJ spins tunes to inspire.

A moose in a tutu, that's truly a sight,
Twirls with a snowflake, oh what a delight!
With laughter and whimsy, they chortle and cheer,
For winter's a party, let's all gather here!

Echoes of a Starry Icy Veil

On a frosty night, my nose turned red,
I shiver and laugh, snuggled in bed.
Snowflakes tickle like a playful tease,
I wonder if penguins wear tiny skis.

A snowball fight with a squirrel so sly,
He throws back acorns, oh me, oh my!
Victory's sweet with a cup of hot cheer,
Coffee's my ally, or so I hold dear.

A Silver Blanket of Night's Embrace

The cold air whispers jokes to the trees,
They chuckle and sway, shivering in breeze.
Icicles hang like a clumsy grin,
Winter's joke is, "Let the fun begin!"

My snowman wears sunglasses, looks quite a sight,
Strutting his stuff in the pale moonlight.
He says, "I'm cool, but my eyes need some shade!"
I laugh so hard at this frosty charade.

Shadows Dancing on the Frosty Ground

The shadows jump, waltzing across the white,
I try to join in, but I fall with a bite.
Penguins are judging from their icy perch,
As I tumble and roll, oh what a lurch!

A snowdog smiles with a carrot for a nose,
He gives me a wink, as his tail he throws.
We make snow angels in a flurry of giggles,
Winter's the season for playful wiggles!

The Chill of Celestial Comfort

The stars are twinkling, playing hide and seek,
While frosty winds make my nose feel weak.
I sip on hot cocoa, marshmallows afloat,
A snowflake lands on my cup, the little goat!

Laughter erupts as I slip on the ice,
A dance of embarrassment, oh isn't this nice?
With the chill in the air, we gather 'round tight,
Tell tales of the moon and its silvery light.

Moonlit Tranquility on the Snowdrift

Snowflakes dance like they're lost,
With frosty fun at any cost.
A snowman winks with frosty eyes,
While squirrels plot their winter lies.

Children giggle, all bundled tight,
As penguins snowball, oh what a sight!
Icicles hang like they might swing,
While winter songs the snowflakes sing.

A rabbit hops with a winter jest,
In boots too big, it's quite the fest.
Hot cocoa spills on mittens bright,
As we laugh beneath the moonlight.

When snowmen melt, there's no remorse,
They'll just be puddles, of course!
Yet laughter echoes, loud and clear,
In this white world, we have no fear.

The Quietude of Frozen Whispers

Whispers float on icy breath,
As snowflakes tumble, flirting with death.
A cat in socks slips on the floor,
Paw prints make a frosty score.

The stars peek out, a cheeky crew,
As if to say, 'We'll join you too!'
A snowball fight, oh what a thrill,
'Til everyone says, 'No more, we're chill!'

Hot soup is served, with laughter brewed,
While snowmen wear our hats—how rude!
The moon shines bright, it seems to snicker,
As we slip and slide, and get much thicker.

As frozen whispers fill the air,
The night laughs back; it's only fair!
Then snuggled warm, we toast for fun,
In this cold dance, we all have won.

Radiant Frost in the Stillness of Night

Frosty windows, a perfect art,
Snowy creations that warm the heart.
An owl hoots with comedic flair,
As snowflakes land on frosty hair.

The moonlight giggles, so full of cheer,
As hot chocolate spills on grandma's sneer.
The trees wear blankets, snug and tight,
In this frosty game, we twiddle all night.

Sledging antics gone tapering wrong,
As winter's chill hums its goofy song.
We tumble down, a flurry of glee,
With frosted noses, it's you and me.

Radiant frost reigns through the sky,
While dreams of spring begin to fly.
So let us laugh, in this cold embrace,
For winter's whim is a merry chase.

Dappled Silver on the White Expanse

The silver glimmers with moonlit beams,
While snowmen scheme up funny dreams.
A pine tree dressed in powdery white,
Sways gently in the soft, nippy night.

As snowballs soar in playful stride,
Even the dogs are caught in pride.
A squirrel shuffles with an acorn stash,
In this whimsical world, we all clash.

When frost bites toes, we dance with glee,
A cha-cha-cha from A to Z.
Giggles echo throughout the glen,
In this winter wonder, we play again.

With dappled silver, we toast our fate,
To funny moments we celebrate.
So let it snow, let laughter soar,
In this chilly world, we ask for more.

Silent Frosted Whispers

Snowflakes dance in a silly twirl,
Making snowmen with a snowy swirl.
The rabbit hops in boots too big,
While penguins slide, doing a jig.

Hot cocoa spills like jokes well told,
The tales of winter never get old.
A squirrel holds acorns like a prize,
With a festive hat that's quite a surprise.

Icicles drip like giggles at night,
As snowflakes tickle with pure delight.
A snowball fight with a sneaky twist,
You'll never guess who's on whose list!

So gather round for this winter cheer,
With laughter echoing loud and clear.
The chilly nights bring warmth so bright,
In the frosted air, we'll share our light.

The Night's Gentle Embrace

Beneath the stars, we laugh and play,
As frosty winds blow worries away.
The moon grins wide, a silly sight,
While snowmen wink in the pale moonlight.

A cat in boots struts through the snow,
While ducks in scarves steal the show.
The crunching crust beneath our feet,
Is like the rhythm of a funky beat.

Snowflakes land on noses with glee,
Transforming us into a sight to see.
The chill can't snuff our cheerful song,
In cozy hats, we all belong.

So let's embrace this frosty air,
With silly stories that we all share.
In the calm of night, we'll find our fun,
As laughter dances with everyone.

Luminous Shadows of December

Flashlights flicker in playful glee,
As shadows dance beneath the tree.
Twinkling lights adorned in every hue,
Make the dark a laughing view.

A snowball rolled becomes a cat,
With fluffy ears and a funny hat.
The neighbors laugh, a sight to see,
As reindeer prance with silly glee.

Frozen ponds hold secrets untold,
While kids in mittens act quite bold.
A slip, a slide, a tumble down,
Laughter echoes all around town.

So join the fun in this frosty play,
Where joy finds a home on a chilly day.
In luminous shadows, we cheer and shout,
As December brings what winter's about!

Echoes Beneath the Silver Veil

Whispers of jokes ride the chilly breeze,
As chuckles chase the shivering trees.
A snowman with a carrot nose,
Holds secrets that nobody knows.

Frosted cupcakes line the festive table,
With sprinkles that dance, so colorful and able.
A cat in mittens steals a treat,
Dashing away on glittery feet.

In shadows deep, the mischief brews,
While giggles echo, it's a joyous muse.
A fireplace crackles with stories great,
Of penguin parties we can't relate.

So let's toast to this winter's jest,
With laughter and joy, we are truly blessed.
In silver veils where snowflakes swirl,
We'll keep the fun in our frosty world.

Dreaming Beneath the Icy Veil

Snowflakes fall with grace,
As squirrels dance in place.
If only they could know,
That winter's like a show!

Hot cocoa spills, oh dear,
The marshmallows disappear.
I slip on icy ground,
And hear my laughter sound!

Crazy hats and mittens,
With funny patterns written.
We juggle oranges bright,
In the frosty moonlight!

Chasing snowmen that run,
Wishing we could have fun.
The winter's quite a tease,
With cold winds that don't freeze!

Luminous Threads in the Winter's Grasp

Icicles hanging high,
They shimmer, oh so sly.
I trip and slip, not cool,
Gathering snow like a fool!

With snowballs set to fly,
We toss but hear a cry.
A snowman's smile so wide,
He guards our snowy slide!

Dancing dogs with glee,
Chasing snowflakes like spree.
Wearing sweaters too tight,
In this chilly delight!

We cozy up with tea,
Like penguins, oh so free.
For laughter rules the night,
In frosty, silly light!

Softly Glowing in the Wintry Night

Blankets piled so high,
We giggle and then sigh.
The wind sings lullabies,
With twinkling starry eyes!

Furry slippers, what a sight,
They make our toes feel right.
We dance around the fire,
While sipping cocoa higher!

Snowflakes tickle our nose,
Each little one just goes.
Through the air, they glide down,
Wearing winter's pure gown!

With our friends and delight,
The world's a snowy white.
Underneath the chill's breath,
We laugh like there's no death!

Gleaming Memories of Frostbitten Times

Remember that cold spree?
When we lost our last tree?
It fell with quite a bang,
Oh, the laughter it sang!

Our snowmen had a fight,
With noses made of fright.
They melted in the sun,
But oh, how we had fun!

Chasing penguins around,
In socks that made no sound.
While umbrellas turned small,
Oh, these frosty mishalls!

We cherish tales like these,
Winter's funny misdeeds.
Through the snow and the chill,
We ride on laughter's thrill!

Shimmers of Light on Snowy Pines

In the silent woods, a snowball flies,
A snowman winks with frosty eyes.
The squirrels dance in fluffy attire,
While the owl just hoots, looking rather tired.

Icicles hang like forgotten spears,
The rabbits laugh, ignoring their fears.
As snowflakes twirl, they trip and fall,
Even the deer join in on the brawl.

A snowflake lands on a frozen nose,
A giggle erupts from their winter prose.
The world is white, yet spirits are bright,
In the shimmers of light, we find delight.

Through the pines, a prankster breeze,
Blowing snowflakes, trying to tease.
Nature chuckles at the playful sight,
As laughter echoes into the night.

Enchanted Silence of the Night

The moon grins widely, a Cheshire Cat,
While penguins slide in a funny spout.
A hush falls soft as snowflakes flit,
Yet a snowman's nose is slightly unfit.

Against the backdrop of darkened skies,
A fox does pirouettes, oh how he tries!
A giggle swells from the frosty ground,
As the critters compete, making joyful sound.

The stars peek out, like curious spies,
Critters dance, wearing no disguise.
In this enchanted hush, we take flight,
Chasing giggles through the velvet night.

What awkward beasts roam in their night glee,
With furry hats and big cups of tea?
Their antics unfold in the moon's soft light,
As laughter twirls in the frosty night.

The Muffled Story of Falling Snow

A plump snowflake trips, then starts to roll,
It lands on a cat, who steals the whole show.
With whiskers frosted, it meows aloud,
While children giggle, hidden in a crowd.

Snowmen gather, plotting their pranks,
They swap their noses, funny little shanks.
A top hat tilts on a snowman's head,
While a bird perches, giggling instead.

In the feathery drift, secrets unfold,
Of snowball fights and tales retold.
Laughter muffled, beneath the white,
As the world spins in a whirl of delight.

Falling snow whispers a soft refrain,
Of snowflakes dancing, each one a mainframe.
Amidst the giggles, a story takes flight,
As we weave through this fluffy night.

A Frosty Canvas of Forgotten Tales

The landscape gleams with a frosty hue,
Old boots stomp softly, how the laughter grew.
With frostbitten fingers, they sculpt and mold,
Giggles erupt as the magic unfolds.

Sleds racing down hills made of gleaming white,
With playful shrieks, pure delight ignites.
A snowball flies, a swift little ghost,
As snowmen break, claiming the post.

The canvas speaks of bygone feet,
Where laughter echoes in rhythmic beat.
Each snowflake a memory, each icicle a tale,
In this frosty realm, humor sets sail.

Whimsical shadows in the moon's embrace,
Chasing snowflakes, a comical race.
Amidst the laughter, the night never fails,
To paint a canvas of whimsical tales.

The Quiet Beauty of Snowflakes' Whirl

Snowflakes tumble down with flair,
Dancing through the chilly air.
They land on dogs that bark and prance,
And cats that plot their latest chance.

A snowman with a carrot nose,
Winks at me as the cold wind blows.
His scarf's too tight, it's plain to see,
He shivers like a leafless tree.

Children's laughter fills the night,
As they launch snowballs with delight.
But watch out for that sneaky one,
Who aims right for your face - oh, fun!

The world's aglow in frosty white,
As snow twists, twirls, and takes flight.
With every flake, we shake and shout,
For the joy of winter leaves no doubt.

Frosted Radiance of the Night Sky

Stars twinkle bright in the frozen dome,
But I'd prefer a warm, cozy home.
The moon is grinning, a snowball fight,
I'll dodge each flake with all my might.

Icicles hang like jagged teeth,
A frozen feast, oh what a treat!
They glisten like jewels on a vine,
But bite one? Oh no, that'd be divine!

Sledding down hills with squeals of glee,
But wait, is that a tree…oh dear me!
For every glide brings joyful cries,
And sometimes a wipeout that defies!

All bundled up, we stomp and swirl,
In this chilly, icy fun-filled whirl.
We laugh, we trip, we dance with grace,
In this frosted world, we've found our place.

Nighttime Whispers in Crystalized Air

The air is crisp, the world's aglow,
With whispers soft, like falling snow.
I trip on ice with a pirate's flair,
Hoping nobody sees my despair!

The frost decorates the starlit ground,
It sparkles, twinkling all around.
Yet every step's a comical scene,
Like a penguin, I waddle so keen!

Hot chocolate waits, its warmth divine,
Yet spill it all, oh what a sign!
Marshmallows float like fluffy dreams,
But sticky fingers? Well, that just seems!

With every giggle, the cold ignites,
As laughter carries through frosty nights.
In this chilled kingdom of slips and slides,
We find our joy, where silliness resides.

Twilight's Embrace on a Frozen Canvas

Dusk settles in, the sun bids adieu,
While I wrap up in layers, too few.
The snow's a canvas, pure and bright,
With my snow angel gone—we'll have a fight!

Footprints mark where I've made my way,
Each step feels like a ballet sway.
But oops! I'm tumbling—a graceful dive,
The locals cheer, "Look! She's alive!"

A snowball whizzes, a head turns fast,
It makes contact, oh what a blast!
Snowflakes cling to my rosy cheeks,
As laughter bursts, and joy peaks.

So here's to the chill and all that it brings,
To frosty smiles and silly flings.
With every giggle, we dance and play,
In the bright embrace of a snowy day!

Echoing Moments in the Frosty Twilight

Snowflakes chuckle as they fall,
A chilly tickle, who could stall?
The squirrels wear jackets, bright and bold,
While penguins slide, their cheeks turn cold.

Frosty breath takes the shape of gnomes,
Caught in laughter, they wander homes.
Hot cocoa sips bring puffs of steam,
As mittens dance with a frosty gleam.

Frost-Crowned Dreams in Crystal Night

Glistening icicles hang like teeth,
The trees wear crowns, oh what a wreath!
A snowman grins with carrot nose,
Giving penguins tips on winter rows.

Sneaky snowballs fly through the air,
Giggling kids, without a care.
They trip and tumble, laughter spills,
While sleds take flight down snowy hills.

Soft Glows Dancing on the Frozen World

The moonlight winks at the frozen ground,
As shadows of rabbits dance around.
Fuzzy boots stomp in rhythmic time,
Marching to winter's silly rhyme.

Hats fly off in a frosty breeze,
As cheerful snowmen bend their knees.
The owls hoot jokes from trees above,
In this frosty world, we find the love.

Luminescent Nightingale in Icy Skies

Nightingales crooned from tree to tree,
With frosty breath, they sing with glee.
The flakes are twinkling, like little stars,
All bundled up in cozy jars.

A penguin struts with a flashy flair,
While rabbits hop, with snow in hair.
They party on till the break of dawn,
In this chill, the laughter lingers on.

Echoes of the Night in Whiteness

Snowflakes dance like silly sprites,
Chasing shadows in the night.
They trip and tumble, all around,
As laughter echoes from the ground.

A snowman grins, with carrot nose,
Wobbles slightly, then he doze.
Frosty friends in winter wear,
Share cheeky jokes without a care.

Fluffy flakes with playful poise,
Make the night a stage for noise.
Even trees sport hats so tall,
Making nature's winter ball.

So grab a sled and slide away,
Join the fun, don't hesitate.
In this chill, we find our groove,
Beneath the moon, we laugh and move.

Serenity Cloaked in Silver

The moon spills secrets, soft and bright,
Over snowmen having a snowball fight.
A squirrel squints at a snow-draped scene,
Wonders if snowflakes are whippy or mean.

Beneath the branches, a snow cat purrs,
Watching winter's mishaps and blurs.
Chimneys puff like angry trolls,
As the wind steals hats from lost souls.

The frozen pond holds a daring rink,
Where ice skates slip, and no one can think.
The frosty air gives all a tickle,
And sledders sprint, trying not to giggle.

Illuminated by a silver sheen,
The world looks comical and serene.
Gather 'round, let's share a toast,
To winter's whimsy, we love the most!

Frosted Lanterns in the Night

Lanterns glow like warm, fuzzy hugs,
As children dash for playful bugs.
Frosted whispers tickle the air,
Turning cheeks rosy, with winter flair.

A penguin waddles, sporting a scarf,
While snowflakes giggle and have a laugh.
The jolly trees sway with delight,
As the snowmen moonwalk through the night.

Puppies in boots chase glittery trails,
Leaving behind their snowy fails.
A snicker here, a chuckle there,
In this frosted wonderland, we share.

With frosted lanterns lighting the way,
We find joy in every playful sway.
Let's dance through the chill, embrace the fun,
In the sparkle of night, we'll never be done!

Shimmering Dreams of a Frosty Glow

A snowflake dreams of a funky dance,
Hoping tonight will give it a chance.
With shimmering sparkles and giggly tunes,
It twirls in the glow of the frosty moon.

The rabbits hop in winter's embrace,
Frolicking freely like they won a race.
They play leapfrog with patches so white,
Creating a flurry of silly delight.

With snowball fights and icicle swords,
The frosty fun shoots through like words.
Ice cubes melt with laughter so bright,
In this wintery world, all feels just right.

Dreams shimmer and dance in the air,
As mischief unfolds without a care.
Let's savor the giggles, the fun, and the cheer,
In winter's embrace, we hold all near.

Dreamscapes of Slumbering Woodlands

The squirrels all play hide and seek,
While bunnies join in for a peek.
Frosty branches wear fluffy hats,
Prancing around like silly cats.

The owls hoot jokes in a wise old way,
With laughter echoing through the day.
Mice moonwalk on a frozen stream,
Chasing shadows like a wild dream.

The brook hums tunes of frozen cheer,
While snowflakes dance without a fear.
Raccoons on stilts, they glide and spin,
Who knew such fun could start with a grin?

As twilight paints the world in gray,
The woodland critters call it a day.
Wrapped in giggles and snowball fights,
Adventures abound through the frosty nights.

Winter's Gentle Breath Across the Land

Icicles hang like chandeliers,
While snowmen float with frosty beers.
Penguins toilet slide down the hill,
Joyful laughter sets the thrill.

The bears wear scarves and twirl with glee,
As they waltz around the old pine tree.
Snowflakes argue on a breezy ride,
One says, "Look, I'm fluffy!" – the other, "I'm wide!"

Chubby rabbits, with noses aglow,
Dig snow forts in a row, row, row.
Frosty mischief fills the air,
While birds on sleds laugh without a care.

As night creeps in, the fireflies dance,
Tiny lights with a mischievous prance.
Sleepy critters bundled tight,
Dreaming of giggles in the night.

Magical Quietude Beneath the Stars

The moon snores softly, a big round ball,
While mice play tag, sometimes they fall.
Stars are winking, shooting across,
Cheering on dreams that never take loss.

Bears in pajamas, comfy and round,
Create snow angels without making a sound.
The owls give eye rolls, wise as can be,
While dreaming of midnight snacks by a tree.

The frozen pond dons a shiny coat,
Where frogs perform in a wintry boat.
Laughter rises, twinkling with mirth,
In the stillness of this frosty earth.

As bedtime stories weave through the chill,
All the woodland creatures stay still.
But every now and then, they just might squeak,
Tales of funny mischief before they sneek!

The Sorcery of a Silvered World

With every snowflake that tumbles down,
The woodland critters don a frown.
Was that a gnome wearing bright green boots?
Or simply a squirrel with wiggly hoots?

With every toss of powdery white,
The trees chuckle at the funny sight.
A hedgehog rolls with a frosty grin,
Challenging friends to join in the spin.

Vampire snowmen in capes so bright,
Chasing the moon through the long winter night.
As magic wafts through the bitter air,
Laughter rings out in a comical flare.

Through the tangle of branches and sparkly frost,
Creatures unite and know there's no cost.
To share in the joy, twinkling under the moon,
In this silvered world, with laughter's tune.

Chilled Dreams of the Midnight Sky

In the night when the ice cream freezes,
The owls wear hats made of cheese,
Snowflakes dance like they've got the moves,
While penguins practice their silly grooves.

Mice in scarves sip on hot cocoa,
Riding sleds made of big marshmallows,
Squirrels throw snowballs with funny aims,
They giggle and laugh, forgetting their names.

Cats are plotting a snowball fight,
With tiny helmets, they take to flight,
Rolling in snow, they make a mess,
How odd, their purrs start to sound like stress.

As moonlight shakes off its frosty chills,
The world erupts in laughter and thrills,
Dreams of sugarplums all must collide,
With giggles and grins, let's all take a ride.

Glacial Serenades of the Heart

The icicles play their glissando tunes,
Underneath the snuggly, floppy spoons,
Penguins line up, they're ready to dance,
With waltzing snowflakes, they take a chance.

Bears wear mittens, so big and so grand,
While rabbits hop 'round in a conga band,
Fluffy white clouds are their stage tonight,
As they prance beneath the shimmering light.

Snowmen sing songs about carrot noses,
While twirling and swaying atop the roses,
Hot chocolate rivers flow, never to freeze,
Creating a backdrop of silly unease.

And as the night wraps in its blanket of blue,
Naps come dressed in pajamas for two,
Shivering giggles erupt into cheer,
For winter's a joke when the fun's drawing near.

Frostbitten Lullabies

Beneath blankets thick, creatures unite,
With stories of mischief woven in white,
Hibernating bears talk of snacks in their dreams,
While snowflakes tickle with giggly beams.

Chipmunks whisper secrets to their acorns,
As frosty breezes deliver their warnings,
Tummies rumble like drums in the night,
With popcorn parties till dawn's early light.

The shivering trees gossip with zest,
About wild snowball fights, we know who's best,
Squirrels are trying to swing from a flake,
Everyone falls, but they're wide awake.

Lullabies echo with a twist of the breeze,
As laughter erupts and begins to tease,
Winter's a canvas where we all take part,
In this frosty playground that tickles the heart.

Whispers of the Pale Horizon

Snowmen giggle in a long, narrow line,
As they share jokes about hot soup and wine,
The chilly moon rolls its bright, funny eyes,
Amidst a concert of pasty snow pies.

Bats in scarves flit as they play night tag,
While snowflakes fall like a fluffy drag,
Trees wear sassy garlands of lights,
As penguins join in on their late-night flights.

The otters slip on the ice with a grin,
Splitting their sides as they tumble, they spin,
Frosty giggles echo from hilltop to hill,
While critters below feel the nighttime thrill.

Night blankets all in a whimsical charm,
With laughter and dances – not a single alarm,
In this icy world where the fun comes alive,
Let's toast to the winter and all who survive!

Shining Whispers of Located Luminance

A snowman dreams of warmer days,
Wishing for sunbeams, sun-soaked rays.
He tries to dance, falls on his nose,
Giggles erupt, where chilly wind blows.

The moonlight chuckles, a playful tease,
As squirrels plan their heist, with stealth and ease.
A nutty banquet set on a branch,
They scamper and slip, oh what a chance!

Icicles dangle, sharp as a blade,
Must be careful where ice grips the glade.
A penguin slips on melted remains,
Elusive grace turns into goofy gains.

The frost tickles noses, bright red and round,
Winter's antics dance on the ground.
With snowflakes fluttering, laughs on the run,
In this chilly chaos, winter's just fun!

The Enigma of Frosty Dawn

A cat in boots, tiptoes through snow,
Chasing its tail, putting on a show.
With each spin, it falls on its back,
Meows for help, but that's just an act!

The coffee pot's frozen, what a bizarre scene,
While penguins form line at the local cuisine.
They order fish cakes while wiggling their feet,
Just trying to keep warm, find something to eat.

The snowflakes giggle as they splash from the skies,
Some land in eyes, a hilarious surprise.
A snowball flies, hits a man with a beard,
He laughs so loud, it's utterly weird!

Frosty trees laugh, they look like fine jesters,
With branches adorned in icy ballisters.
As dawn sneaks in, the world looks so bright,
A quirky start to this wintry delight!

Lunar Reflections in Crystal Clarity

Beneath the glow of silver light,
The snowflakes dance in sheer delight.
Squirrels wearing hats made of cheese,
Offer acorns to the chilly breeze.

The moon's a cookie in the sky,
As penguins waddle by and sigh.
A snowman shimmies, tries to groove,
But slips and lands, in quite the move.

Icicles hang like frozen spears,
Beasts play hockey, sharing cheers.
Hares in scarves throw snowballs wide,
While owls hoot, with snowy pride.

The world is wrapped in silly cheer,
With laughter echoing, oh so clear.
A sparkling night of frosty fun,
Beneath the moon, we laugh and run.

Emptiness Wrapped in Snow

The empty streets just wait and yawn,
As laughter breaks the frosty dawn.
A snowman named Ted tells jokes,
While frosty friends share giggling pokes.

A snowball fight breaks out with glee,
But someone grabs a cup of tea.
"Let's keep this battle clean," they shout,
As chocolate bombs fly all about!

The world feels soft, like cotton candy,
People slip 'cause they're just dandy.
Frogs in boots laugh as they schmooze,
Making snowmen in bright, bold hues.

But when the sun begins to shine,
Their playful spirits intertwine.
With snowflakes melting, they still play,
With silly smiles that call for day.

Twilight's Breath on Icy Windows

Twilight whispers in shades of blue,
Porch lights flicker, a glimmering view.
Cats in coats prance on icy paths,
While the moon giggles and shares its laughs.

Windows fogged, a swirly scene,
The dogs debate who's the best queen.
With noses pressed, they all peek out,
At snowmen selfies, with a shout!

Chickens in boots dance in a ring,
Holding signs that declare it's spring!
But winter chuckles and stays a while,
Their frosty faces wearing a smile.

A snowflake slips on a banana peel,
Causing snowfolk to spin and reel.
Yet with each tumble and silly fall,
Echoes of laughter reign over all.

The Soft Glow of Quiet Repose

In a blanket of white lies the world at ease,
With quiet chuckles from the trees.
A friendly fox in a fuzzy hat,
Does the cha-cha with a sneaky cat.

The stars poke fun at chilly nights,
While rabbits zoom on their snowy flights.
Unicorns prance with cups of tea,
Winking at snowflakes, wild and free.

The moon lies back with a face so round,
As winter's crew gathers 'round.
Mice in boots call for popcorn snacks,
While snowballs fly in friendly attacks.

With laughter blending, a cozy glow,
In the soft glow of falling snow.
They share their tales, both big and small,
In this enchanted winter ball.

Silver Haze Over a Dreaming World

In silver fog, the world skips by,
Snowmen dance, under a starry sky.
They jig in boots, with hats askew,
While penguins plot a ski resort too.

Bunnies in scarves throw snowball darts,
But carrots vanish, oh where are their parts?
Laughs echo as they tumble around,
In this snowy land where joy abounds.

Fluffy clouds serve marshmallow treats,
While squirrels host wild winter feats.
Chasing their tails in gleeful ballet,
Winter's charm keeps the blues at bay.

As frostbite nips at toes and noses,
Laughter erupts, in flurries and poses.
In a world wrapped in gleaming white,
Winter giggles dance into the night.

Beneath a Shroud of Winter's Light

The moon peeks in and sings its tune,
A snowflake falls and reads a rune.
Pigeons wear sweaters, all mismatched,
While children giggle, their noses scratched.

Penguins waddle, with quite the flair,
While snowflakes tickle, here and there.
With ice cream cones made out of ice,
They serve up laughs, oh isn't it nice?

Bells chime softly from frozen trees,
Rabbits ask, 'Is it time for cheese?'
Hats fly off as they frolic and play,
In this winter realm, they laugh the day.

Chased by shadows of chubby bears,
Hot cocoa spills, while no one cares.
Wrapped snugly in laughter, all merry and bright,
Winter's delight sparkles through the night.

Echoing Lullabies of the Snowy Hills

On snowy hills, the echoes ring,
Of playful pranks and snowball fling.
With muffled giggles beneath their breath,
They frolic on slopes, defying death!

Frosty trees wear their winter caps,
Twirling and swirling in friendly laps.
Sleds zoom by with a squeal and grin,
As playful races fill with win.

Snowflakes swirl around happy cheers,
While hot cocoa warms the winter fears.
Snow angels spread their wings with glee,
As snowmen toast, "Just let it be!"

Frosted trails lead to jolly fun,
As everyone joins in, one by one.
In a world of laughter, joy takes flight,
In the winter magic, all feels right.

Luminescent Silence on Swirling Clouds

On swirling clouds, the moonlight beams,
Whimsical creatures weave their dreams.
With hats on penguins and socks on bears,
They juggle snowballs, with silly flares.

Chocolate rivers flow, oh what a sight!
Where marshmallow ducks take flight at night.
Giggling elves ride on frosty steeds,
While snowmen plant their frosty seeds.

Dancing shadows skip across the snow,
With comical prances, they steal the show.
A winter circus unfolds near the pines,
As laughter echoes in magical lines.

In a world where humor reigns supreme,
Each snowflake's a trick, a hilarious scheme.
Beneath the glow of a friendly moon,
Winter's charm keeps us grinning soon.

Silhouettes Beneath the Icy Light

Snowmen stand with carrot noses,
While frozen toes dance on their toes.
A penguin slides, gives a cheeky wink,
And squirrels plot, with nuts on the brink.

Frosty breath makes clouds like dreams,
Giggling children, or so it seems.
They toss snowballs, laugh with glee,
All while trying to catch a bee!

Puffs of air like soap-bubble flares,
Elves in hats make snow-doughnut layers.
A snowball fight turns into a race,
As laughter echoes in this frosty space.

With twinkling lights on trees up high,
Reindeer fly with a wink and a sigh.
In this chill, mischief reigns supreme,
As all enjoy this icy dream!

Celestial Whispers in the Stillness

Stars giggle above, twinkling bright,
While the moon plays hide and seek at night.
A snowflake lands on a cat's cold nose,
Startled, it leaps with a hiccuped pose!

Jingle bells jangle with tunes so sweet,
But the neighbor's dog knows just how to cheat.
He sneaks in snowmen, adds silly hats,
Then rolls away with giggly spats!

Mittens chase as kids lose their way,
Their laughter covers the ground like hay.
In a flurry of fun, they dance and spin,
Until someone's sock falls right in the bin!

While snowflakes swirl like tiny chefs,
Making winter cakes from our frozen breaths.
With sugar sprinkles across the ground,
Who knew winter could be so round?

Glistening Shadows on Snowy Mornings

Morning sparkles, a shimmering glow,
While socks go missing in fresh, white snow.
Coffee spills as the mugs find their place,
In the mad rush of winter's embrace!

A dog in boots prances, looking quite slick,
Chasing his tail, oh, what a funny trick!
Snowballs fly, and giggles are loud,
As everyone slips, feeling so proud!

Hot cocoa swirls with marshmallow fluff,
Brave snowflakes will never say 'enough.'
They land on noses, causing big sneezes,
Winter's laughter comes in frosty breezes!

The sun peeks out, oh, what a sight,
While snowflakes dance in a chilly flight.
With frosty breath and cheeks so red,
It's hard not to smile while staying in bed!

Serene Nightfall in Chilling Hues

Evening falls with a soft, chilly air,
While snowmen wear pajamas with flair.
Rabbits hop in moonlight's soft gleam,
Leaving tiny paw prints that dance and beam!

The sound of icicles like wind chimes ring,
While penguins debate whether to sing.
Their flippers flap, creating a show,
With all kinds of dances, oh, don't be slow!

A cozy blanket with laughter wraps tight,
As sleds race down hills, what a delight!
Hot soup simmers, its smell fills the air,
Mismatched socks, but no one can care!

While owls up high hoot out riddles,
Snowflakes spin like whimsical fiddles.
Each moment a giggle, a tale to tell,
As winter dreams weave their frosty spell!

Shadows in a Chilled Embrace

In the frosty air, I trip and fall,
My snowman laughs, a jolly ball.
He wobbles wide, a lopsided grin,
Oh, the joy found in my icy sin!

The squirrels chuckle in their nests,
While snowflakes play their playful quests.
With mittens stuck to my nose so red,
I chase my hat; it's off, it fled!

A penguin slides, wants to join the chase,
We spin and tumble in this cold place.
Laughter bursts, it's contagious, you see,
Even the trees dance, so wild and free!

The moon's a grin, in a snowy attire,
As laughter soars like a warm bonfire.
So here we play, in jumbled noise,
Winter's icy fun, oh what joys!

The Serenity of a Shimmering Winter's Night

Twinkling stars wink like sneaky eyes,
While I juggle snowballs, oh, what a surprise!
But alas, my aim's gone all awry,
Snowflakes splatter, and I hear a sigh!

A cat in a scarf thinks it's a game,
As I slip on ice, feeling so lame.
With flurries dancing, I bumble and stumble,
A comedy show, as my friends all tumble!

The air's a chilly, giggly delight,
Laughter echoes through the frosty night.
Hot cocoa spills as we frolic and play,
Who knew winter nights were so goofy and gay?

So gather 'round, let's create some cheer,
A snowy dance; let's all draw near.
With every slip, we find pure delight,
In this whimsical frolic, that feels so right!

Frosted Reflections in a Night of Tranquility

I wear a hat that's far too big,
And fashion it cool, like a dancing twig.
But when the wind gives a cheeky shove,
It flies away, just like a dove!

The ice is slippery, my footing's unsure,
But giggles escape as I try to endure.
With each little slip, my friends laugh loud,
These frosted moments, I'm oh-so-proud!

A snowflake tickles my nose so bright,
As I try to catch it, what a silly sight!
Snow angels yell, "Up in the air!"
As we tumble together, with nary a care.

So let's toast to the giggle-filled night,
With cocoa mugs raised, oh what a sight!
In a world turned white, we choose to play,
With laughter and smiles, we'll warm this day!

A Dance Beneath the Starlit Chill

We waltz and twirl on frosty ground,
Boots clatter with a ridiculous sound.
The moonlight sparkles like a disco ball,
While we stumble and trip—then we laugh through it all!

Snowmen take photos, they're our fans,
While penguins slide by, plotting new plans.
Here's to the joy of slipping in style,
With every snowy fall, comes a cheeky smile!

The chilly breeze brings a shivery thrill,
As we dance with the laughter, oh what a skill!
Chasing frostbite, but with hearts full of glee,
In the midst of this winter, we're wild and free!

So come join the fun, leave your worries behind,
In this frosty wonderland, let's unwind.
As stars shine bright in the chilled sky so still,
We'll laugh and dance, for it's winter's thrill!

Glimmers of Hope in a Frozen Landscape

In the snow, I saw a cat,
Wearing boots, imagine that!
It slid and danced with such great flair,
Chasing snowflakes through the air.

The trees are draped in frosty white,
While squirrels hide their snacks from sight.
One jumped high and missed the branch,
Fell in a pile that made me chanch!

A snowman wore a carrot nose,
But forgot how to wear its clothes.
With buttons missing, it looked shy,
Still waving at the passersby.

The chilly wind whistled a tune,
As penguins waddled to the moon.
They danced the salsa, quite absurd,
In a snowy world, so undeterred.

Winter's Heartbeat Beneath a Soft Glow

The stars above, they twinkle bright,
While snowflakes spark like diamonds light.
A bunny hops with stylish flair,
In a tiny scarf, it shows its care.

The whispers of the snowflakes sing,
As kids make snowballs, laughing, fling.
One hit a man—oh, what a sight!
Who yelled, aghast, "That's not polite!"

A frozen pond, with skaters bold,
Spinning tales that must be told.
One lost a boot on the slide,
As laughter echoed far and wide.

And then a snowdog came to play,
Chasing shadows, leading the way.
With a wagging tail and frosty beard,
It joined the dance, not one person steered!

Nightride Through Shimmering Snow

On a sled, I took my seat,
But oh dear, what a chilly feat!
We zoomed down slopes, oh what a sight,
Squealing like banshees, hearts took flight!

The moonlit path was slick and bright,
With snowmen peeking, what a fright!
One bald and round—a missing hat,
Looked like it'd been in a spat!

The dogs ran fast, with tongues a-flap,
Chasing snowflakes in a lively trap.
They tripped and tumbled in the white,
Making more fun on this chilly night!

Then came the snowball war of fate,
Dodging pelts, there was great debate.
With giggles shared, the battle ceased,
As friends now formed a snowman feast!

When Silence Falls on Frostbitten Fields

The fields are white with quiet grace,
But snowmen plot a sneaky chase.
They gather round, with eyes of coal,
In the moonlight, they start to troll!

A snowball flung, a target hit,
As giggles spark, we can't admit.
We hide behind a mound of snow,
Waiting for more mischievous flow!

A hedgehog rolled like a tiny ball,
Through the drifts, it made its call.
With tiny paws and spiky sprees,
It tangled with the wind, with ease!

And in the night, the laughter swells,
As toppled snowmen bid farewell.
With hearts so light, and cheeks aglow,
We'll dance in dreams, till the sun shows!

The Frost-Kissed Lullaby

Snowflakes dance on noses small,
As penguins waddle, heads held tall.
In cozy socks, we spin and swirl,
The chill escapes with every twirl.

Hot cocoa spills, oh what a sight,
Mittens gone, our hands in flight.
With marshmallows floating all around,
We laugh so hard, we can't hold sound.

Outdoors we play in fluff so white,
Making angels 'til the night.
With sleds we race from hill to hill,
The laughter echoes, what a thrill!

As stars peek out from skies of gray,
We dream of sunny days to play.
But for now, we twiddle and hum,
In frosty fun, so much to come!

Moonlit Echoes on Frozen Streams

A shiny moon on icy streams,
Look, that fish has funny dreams!
It jumps, it flips, but then it falls,
And smacks its head in snowy squalls.

Frogs in hats croak silly tunes,
While snowmen dance beneath the moons.
With carrots pointing in their eyes,
They wink and shuffle, oh, what a surprise!

From frosty trees, the icicles swing,
As squirrels hold a winter fling.
They do the cha-cha, slip and slide,
While giggles echo far and wide.

Beneath the stars, we share some pie,
While snowflakes fall, we laugh and cry.
This chilly world wraps us so tight,
With memories warm, we take delight.

Radiance of the Crystal Sky

A crystal sky with sparkly beams,
The snowmen smile, or so it seems.
While frostbite lurks with chilly grins,
We build snow forts and throw some wins.

Sledding down the hills so fast,
All our worries fade, they're past.
But wait! What's that? A tumble and roll!
Our laughter soars, we've lost control.

Icicles dangle, like pointy teeth,
As we spy snowflakes fall beneath.
With every flake, a tale unfolds,
Of winter's secrets and giggles bold.

The night is bright with frosty cheer,
As we sip warm drinks and shed a tear.
For winter's jest will soon play through,
With joys we share, and dreams anew.

Silent Frostings on Whispering Winds

Softly shrubs in white attire,
The trees laugh with a hoot and tire.
They whisper tales of frosty quest,
As kids tumble in their winter vest.

A squirrel darts, the dog gives chase,
Through drifted snow, in a silly race.
But watch out, pup, for airs so cool,
You might just end up in a snow-filled pool!

The moon's a grin, so big and round,
While snowflakes pirouette to the ground.
In this frosty ballet, we find our groove,
With ticklish toes, we dance and move.

As night rolls in, our cheeks are red,
With snowy caps upon our head.
We gather near with tales of cheer,
In winter's laughter, joy appears.

Milton Keynes UK
Ingram Content Group UK Ltd.
UKHW022340171124
451242UK00007B/68

9 789916 945902